P9-BZA-106

Weekly Reader Books Presents

# HATTIE, TOM,
## and the
# CHICKEN WITCH
### An Easter play and story

# by Dick Gackenbach

An I CAN READ Book®

HARPER & ROW, PUBLISHERS

This book is a presentation of Weekly Reader Books.
Weekly Reader Books offers book clubs for children from
preschool through high school. For further information
write to: **Weekly Reader Books,** 4343 Equity Drive,
Columbus, Ohio 43228.

Published by arrangement with Harper & Row, Publishers,
Inc. Weekly Reader is a federally registered trademark of
Field Publications. I Can Read Book is a registered
trademark of Harper & Row, Publishers, Inc.

Hattie, Tom, and the Chicken Witch
Copyright © 1980 by Dick Gackenbach

All rights reserved. No part of this book may be
used or reproduced in any manner whatsoever without
written permission except in the case of brief quotations
embodied in critical articles and reviews. Printed in
the United States of America. For information address
Harper & Row, Publishers, Inc., 10 East 53rd Street,
New York, N.Y. 10022. Published simultaneously in
Canada by Fitzhenry & Whiteside Limited, Toronto.

Library of Congress Cataloging in Publication Data
Gackenbach, Dick.
    Hattie, Tom, and the chicken witch.

    (An I can read book)
    SUMMARY: Hattie Rabbit tries to get a part in Tom's
Easter play. Play script is included.
    [1. Easter stories.   2. Easter—Drama.   3. Plays]
I. Title.
PZ7.G117Hati        [E]        79-2742
ISBN 0-06-021958-0
ISBN 0-06-021959-9 lib. bdg.

**For my mother**

# WHAT? NO RABBIT?

Hattie Rabbit

and her good friend Linda Chicken

were walking.

"Easter will soon be here,"

said Hattie.

"Yes," said Linda.

"Easter is special."

"My Uncle

is the Easter Rabbit,"

said Hattie.

"Easter Rabbit, Easter Rabbit,"

said Linda.

"That is all I hear

at Eastertime.

Why not Easter Chicken?"

"Nonsense," said Hattie.

WANTED
DOGS,
CHICKENS,
AND PIGS
TO
ACT IN
EASTER PLAY.
SEE
TOM RABBIT.

"Look," said Linda.

"There is a sign on that tree."

"So there is," said Hattie.

"Let's see what it says."

Hattie read out loud.

WANTED: DOGS, CHICKENS,

AND PIGS TO ACT

IN EASTER PLAY.

SEE TOM RABBIT.

"I am going to see Tom,"

said Linda.

"I want a part in the play."

Linda hurried away.

Hattie read the sign again.

"There is no rabbit

in that play," Hattie said.

"It must be some mistake.

I will tell Tom so."

WANTED
DOGS
CHICKENS
AND PIGS
TO
ACT IN
EASTER PLAY
SEE
TOM RABBIT

Hattie went to the theater.

She knocked on the door.

"What do you want?"

asked a pig.

"I want to see Tom,"

said Hattie.

"About the play?"

the pig wanted to know.

"Yes," said Hattie.

"No rabbits!"

said the pig.

"Go away!"

Hattie was angry.

She ran home

and went up to the attic.

She found a chicken costume

from Halloween.

Hattie put the chicken costume on.

"It still fits," she said.

Hattie went back to the theater.

This time,

the pig let Hattie in.

"Come in, Chicken," said the pig.

Hattie looked for Tom.

She looked in the balcony.

She looked in the dressing room.

She looked onstage.

There was Tom.

"Hey Tom," shouted Hattie.

"I'm sorry," said Tom.

"The chicken parts are gone."

"I am no chicken," said Hattie.

"I am Hattie!"

"Oh, Hattie," said Tom.

"There are no parts

for rabbits either."

"That is why

I want to see you," said Hattie.

"You cannot do an Easter play

without a rabbit."

"Why not?" asked Tom.

"Because," said Hattie,

"rabbits and Easter

go together.

Like peaches and pits.

Like peanut butter and jelly."

"Well," said Tom,

"we could use a rabbit,

if you do what you are told."

"Okay," said Hattie.

So each day

Hattie came to the theater.

She worked hard.

She did what she was told.

She cleaned the stage curtain.

She made the costumes.

She swept the dirty floor.

But she did not

get a part in the play.

Tom gave Linda

the part called Storyteller.

"That is a good part,"

Hattie told Linda.

"But it should be

a part for a rabbit."

"That is what *you* say," said Linda.

15

Soon it was opening day.

Hattie had nothing to do.

She watched

everyone get ready.

"Where is my wig?"

shouted a chicken.

"How do I look?"

a dog asked.

"Curtain up in three minutes,"

shouted a pig.

"Has anyone seen Linda?"

Tom wanted to know.

The bright lights went on.

The band started to play.

"Where is Linda?"

someone called again.

The audience was waiting.

"Everybody in their places,"

said Tom.

"But where is Linda?"

Then a duck brought Tom a note.

It was from Linda.

*Dear Tom,*

*I fell off my skateboard.*

*I hurt my ankle.*

*Yours truly, Linda.*

"Oh no," cried Tom.

"No Storyteller,

no play."

"I know the part,"

said Hattie.

"No kidding?" said Tom.

"Sure," said Hattie.

"The part was made

for a rabbit."

Tom hugged Hattie.

"The part is yours," he said.

"Good luck."

Hattie took her place onstage.

The music stopped.

The lights dimmed.

The curtain parted.

Hattie began:

"Once upon a time."

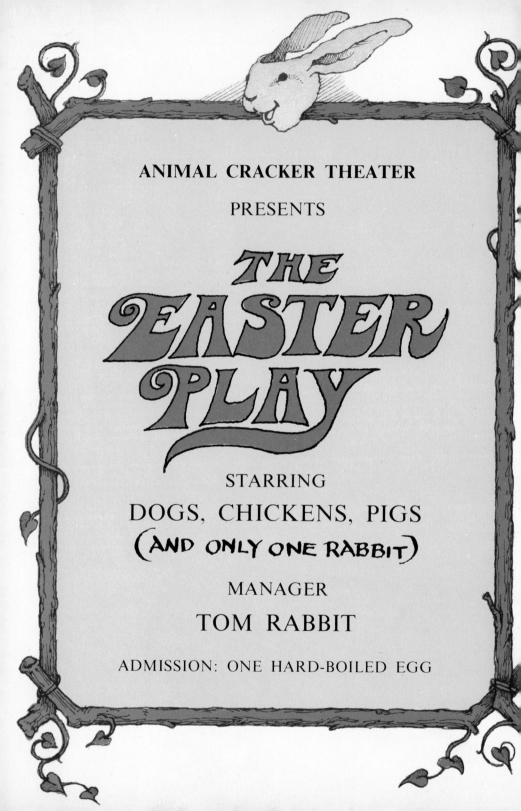

ANIMAL CRACKER THEATER

PRESENTS

# THE EASTER PLAY

STARRING

## DOGS, CHICKENS, PIGS

### (AND ONLY ONE RABBIT)

MANAGER

## TOM RABBIT

ADMISSION: ONE HARD-BOILED EGG

CAST OF PLAYERS

FLO
BRENDA } *Hens*
DARLENE

CAPTAIN DAN, *The Fried-Egg Man*
CHICKEN LICKEN, *A Witch*
TWO EGG COLLECTORS
A STORYTELLER

TIME

THREE DAYS BEFORE EASTER

PLACE

A CHICKEN COOP

SPECIAL EFFECTS

BELLS · COCK-A-DOODLE-DOO
KNOCK · TICK-TOCK

AT RISE

STORYTELLER AT STAGE LEFT,
THREE HENS, CENTER STAGE

STORYTELLER: Once upon a time

when Easter eggs

were plain and white,

hens everywhere

made a promise.

"Captain Dan,"

the hens told

The Fried-Egg Man,

"you can take all the eggs you want."

At first all went well.

But soon

Captain Dan wanted

each and every egg.

24

"My fried eggs are famous,"

he said.

"I want every egg you lay.

A promise is a promise."

FLO: What shall we do?

We have no eggs for cake.

And worse than that,

we have no eggs for Easter.

BRENDA: There are no eggs

to fill the baskets.

DARLENE: There are no eggs

to hide and hunt.

26

FLO: I have a plan.

Come close!

*(Hens huddle together.)*

We will hide half

of all our eggs

for Easter.

Hide some under

our nests.

Hide some

behind the chair.

Hide some

under our bed.

27

STORYTELLER: That night

the hens hide their eggs.

When all the eggs

are tucked in secret places,

the tired hens

fall sound asleep.

Next morning,

the sun rises

and the cock crows.

*(Cock-a-doodle-doo offstage.)*

Then there is

a loud knock on the door.

*(Knock-knock offstage.)*

28

FLO: Wake up, sisters.

It is Captain Dan,

The Fried-Egg Man.

*(Enter Dan and Egg Collectors.)*

DAN: Rise and shine, chickens.

Gather the eggs, boys.

EGG COLLECTORS (gathering eggs):

Eggs! Pile them high!

Eggs are laid for Dan to fry.

STORYTELLER: The hens watch

and hold their breath.

Will Dan find their eggs?

DAN *(counting eggs):*

STOP! NOBODY MOVE!

Something is different

this morning.

I count only half

the number of eggs.

Where are the other eggs?

31

FLO: You counted wrong.

We have no more eggs.

DAN: Never trust a chicken.

Search the coop, boys.

STORYTELLER: The collectors

begin to search.

They look in every

nook and cranny.

One by one,

they find each hidden egg.

DAN: Silly hens,

I am too smart for you.

HENS: Please,

do not take our eggs.

They are for children.

They are for baskets

and egg hunts.

DAN: Phooey on children.

Phooey on baskets.

And double phooey

on egg hunts.

Your eggs belong to me.

Remember your promise.

EGG COLLECTORS: Silly clucks,

sit on your hay.

34

We will come back tomorrow

for every egg you lay.

STORYTELLER: All that day

the hens sit on their nests.

They fuss and cluck.

How can they save the eggs

from Dan's

hot and sizzling pan?

35

FLO: I have another plan.

DARLENE: I hope it works
better than the last plan.

FLO: It will.

I think we should call
on Chicken Licken.

BRENDA: Chicken Licken
is a powerful witch.

DARLENE: A superwitch.

FLO: Do we agree?

Do we call Chicken Licken?

BRENDA and DARLENE: We agree.

FLO: Good.

We will call for bells.

Only ringing bells

can bring us Chicken Licken.

STORYTELLER: The hens

hold hands.

They make a circle.

Slowly they turn.

The chant begins.

37

HENS: Come to us,

O Chicken Licken.

Come by bus.

Come by star.

Come by broomstick.

Come by car.

Break through time.

Zoom through space.

Listen for bells

to find this place.

STORYTELLER: Only sounds

of ringing bells can bring

Chicken Licken to the hens.

If you have a bell,

please help the hens.

Ready—on the count of three.

Jingle, jangle,

one, two, three.

*(Bells ring.*

*Enter Chicken Licken.)*

CHICKEN LICKEN: Did someone

ring for a witch?

Does someone want

three wishes

or a pocket of gold?

FLO: No, nothing like that.

CHICKEN LICKEN: Wonderful!

I hate those old tricks.

What do you want?

DARLENE: Save our eggs.

Greedy Captain Dan

takes all the eggs we lay.

He fries them

in his hot

and sizzling pan.

41

BRENDA: We have

no eggs for Easter.

No eggs for baskets.

No eggs to hide

on garden lawns.

What shall we do?

CHICKEN LICKEN:

Hide them!

FLO: We tried that.

It did not work.

CHICKEN LICKEN: This job

calls for the Clever Hat.

*(Witch pulls hat from bag of tricks.)*

There! See!

I am clever already.

An idea has begun to tick.

Listen! Hear it?

*(Tick-tock, tick-tock offstage.)*

And oh,

what a lovely idea it is.

We need magic.

Not plain magic,

mind you,

but color magic.

I have everything

in my Trick Bag.

See!

Yellows! Blues! Reds!

Brushes too.

Now, paint your eggs

in pretty plaids.

Dot them with polka dots.

Cover them with stripes.

STORYTELLER: All night long,

the hens paint eggs.

In the morning,

the plain white eggs

are fancy and colorful.

FLO: The eggs are beautiful.

BRENDA: The children

will love them.

DARLENE: But are they safe

from greedy Captain Dan?

Where shall we hide them?

CHICKEN LICKEN: You do not

need to hide the eggs.

46

Captain Dan will see

only plaids

and dots

and stripes.

He will never know

they are eggs.

*(Cock-a-doodle-doo offstage.)*

FLO: It is morning.

Captain Dan

will soon be here.

CHICKEN LICKEN: I will go

to every chicken coop

and tell every hen

to paint her eggs.

Send me on my way

with sounds of bells.

STORYTELLER: Everyone

who has a bell, ready now.

On the count of three.

Jingle, jangle,

one, two, three.

*(Bells ring. Exit Chicken Licken.)*

Now the three hens
are happy.

They begin to dance.

Happy Easter thoughts
fill their heads.

50

But their happiness

does not last long.

*(A loud knock-knock offstage.)*

HENS: It is Captain Dan,

The Fried-Egg Man.

*(Hens huddle together.*

*Enter Dan and Collectors.)*

DAN: I hope

you silly birds

did not hide

your eggs

again.

51

EGG COLLECTORS: Dan is no dope.

He is wise.

He gets a nickel

for each egg he fries.

FLO: There are no eggs today.

We could not lay

a single egg.

DARLENE: It must be the weather.

DAN: The weather, my eye.

You are up to tricks again.

BRENDA: Look for yourself.

DAN: You can bet your feathers

I will.

Find the eggs, boys.

STORYTELLER: The collectors

search the coop

from top to bottom,

inside out

and upside down.

EGG COLLECTORS: We find plaids

behind the chair.

There are stripes

everywhere.

Lots of dots

we can see.

But not one egg

there seems to be.

DAN: Rotten luck!

On to the next coop.

If we do not find eggs,

I am ruined.

*(Exit Dan and his gang.)*

FLO: No more eggs

for Captain Dan.

Hurray for Easter!

56

BRENDA: Hurray for baskets!

DARLENE: Hurray for egg hunts!

STORYTELLER: That Easter

was the best Easter

the hens ever had.

The colorful eggs

made the children

very happy.

From then on,

the hens always

colored their Easter eggs.

But what happened

to greedy Captain Dan?

Why, Dan became

The Fried-Potato Man.

The potato was easy to fry.

It was always there

when Dan wanted it.

And he didn't have to worry

about tricky chickens.

## BRAVO, HATTIE

The curtain closed.

The play was over.

Hattie took a bow.

"BRAVO, HATTIE,"

everyone cheered.

The chickens and dogs

and pigs told Hattie

it was nice to have a rabbit

in the Easter play.

Later,

Tom and Hattie

left the theater together.

"I think we should go

to Linda's house,"

Hattie said.

"Let's see how

she is feeling."

"I agree," said Tom.

Hattie and Tom

went to see Linda.

"Is your ankle better?"

Hattie asked.

"Yes," said Linda.

"I am sorry

I was not in the play.

62

But I am glad

Hattie took my place."

"Hattie was great,"

Tom told Linda.

"Is the story

in the play

a true one?"

Linda asked.

"Oh no," said Tom.

"It is only make-believe.

But it does

make a funny play."

"And it also

proves something,"

said Hattie.

"What?"

Linda wanted to know.

"It proves," said Hattie,

"the chicken

is just as important

to Easter

as the rabbit."